ON WINGS OF
LOVE AND LIGHT

Poetry and Essays by

Chris R. Powell & Laura Vosika

Cover photo: Chris R. Powell
Cover design: Laura Vosika

Contact editors@gabrielshornpress.com
Published Minneapolis, MN , Gabriel's Horn Press
First printing: May 11 2021 in the United States.
ISBN-13: 978-1-938990-68-7

Table of Contents

On Wings of Love & Light

FOREWORD

On Wings of Love and Light began as a simple collection of one man's poetry and music, chronologically arranged, but, as we saw the natural progression, it evolved into telling a story through verse. To tell that story, a few poems were removed, a few added, and some essays on love were written.

Make the personal universal, goes an old writing adage, and make the universal personal. We tell a story. Stories are always partly true and partly fiction—to tell deeper truths. Some of the poems were written for reasons that had nothing to do with this book but they fit a theme and a story that is re-told throughout history and we hope you find both the universal and perhaps some of your own personal story in it.

The photography is by Emmanuel's Light, shot in locations around Scotland by Chris R. Powell.

LIFE, DEATH, and LOVE

Imagine. Death. Evolution. Life. True Love. Twice...

I go back to early 2014–two funerals, in two states, my eulogy, I gave—twice. Composed a *Requiem*, and played it live, twice. The tears flowing, truly gushing... Loss. Life... and Love. A path that truly shines, a legacy of love, and...Emilie, our daughter. Thirteen at the time(!), yet receiving a citizenship award from school the semester she lost her mother, because she always was so focused. Her mother was so proud. I mean, *so* proud... Bonnie spent significant time being "there" for Emilie, changing her hours at work in order to *be*...at home, at school, reading to the kids, going on every outing and field trip. She lived longer than she very well should have with the disease. Demons that gripped her final days, because she wanted to remain...*there*, for Emilie, for me, her husband, both of whom she was so proud. A life cut short, yet truly fulfilled, an example of how to live, and exit this life, leaving behind precious commodities, of life, love, and loss.

I wrote the book on her story, which was very cathartic to me. It resolved my Grief (with a capital G) because I was left bereft...my wife of 24 years, simply gone. Her last expression one of wrenching loss, yet her hazel eyes still so beautiful—those eyes that drew me in, Irish eyes, Irish spunk, Irish...love. Emilie was left bereft, of her mother, at the very point a mother is of supreme importance to a young lady growing up—the very edge of 13 going on 14. I have remained her parent—her mother, her father, her Everything. As she hyper-focuses on every aspect of my health and well-being, caring for me, dreading any potential loss or problem, fearing being unable to carry on if I should depart... essentially, Ever. How can she, given that the richest relationship she had was with two parents, together, raising our daughter...her. She was the most beautiful child ever born, three months prematurely. She looked so much like me, the nurse said in the O.R., "You will never be able to deny this child." And indeed, I cannot...yet she rejects a lot of what I try to give because she inherited her mother's Virtue (again, with a capital V).

Now, imagine, again. Mere months later. You are without love...without companionship. You crave what you have lost, in a way that doesn't replace what was lost, but builds on it, taking it higher. Magnifying the life you have just spent the last few months documenting in the book. God is in charge.

And suddenly, there is our Mother Mary, standing beside Bonnie. My beautiful son Ryan Michael, who died at birth, is in his mother's arms, smiling beatifically at me.

Wait, *what*? We were Baptists! This Mother Mary concept...what?

And yet, I was returning Home. The faith of this perfect future companion was an example, reminding me of how my father joined my mother in her Catholic faith. I followed my father's example, and yet, this true example of Heavenly faith and following, my Laura (eventually...) was there, and so was Bonnie, and Ryan Michael, and...Our Mother Mary. So soon, and yet, so right. The future, but the past also, and, well, *everything*. Family, first and foremost. Love, right there next to Family. A legacy, of carrying on, and carrying through. Raphael and Uriel, standing in light with my Love, showing that there was a path from betrayal and terror, after taking a turn into a true "dumpster fire."

Lessons have been learned: Of devotion, peace, family, faith, contemplation, and, most of all, true Love. Of God, of Bonnie, and of Laura. True love, twice.... With a sinner, a lost soul, a father, a son, a husband, and, well, love, being, yet denying, moving, yet stumbling, always with true Love shining its light, through Hawk, Eagle, and Swan. Such symbols...such Love, such necessity. Such humility...

To be given the gift of Life and Love, twice in one's journey, is a remarkable gift. I have been bestowed such blessing. I have Bonnie and Laura to thank for it.

And, Emilie, my eternal heart.

Requiem

May 2, 2014

Bonnie died on December 29, 2013 at the age of 48.
We had been married 24 -1/2 years.

Requiem was a last act of love, written for her and performed at her two memorial services.

It can be found on Chris's YouTube channel:

https://tinyurl.com/chrisrpowellrequiem
OR
https://bit.ly/3t3ixND

MEETING

Kiss You Every Morning

Early 2014

A song

(Chorus)
(Bb, lyric starting on Bb) I need to kiss you in the morning
(F, lyric starting on A) I need to kiss you every night
(Eb, lyric starting on G) I need to feel that you are near me
(Bb, lyric starting on Bb) Every day and every night

(Verses generally follow pattern above)

A new day has dawned for me
The sign of our Father's Holy light
The sun through the windows
Brightens my entire life

Your head on the pillow
Your eyes take in the sight
You smile in the sunshine
And it pulls back every night
(Chorus)

There is a prayer of gladness
Arising from my heart
I say a prayer of Thanksgiving
Every day at the start

Take a walk in the daylight
Your head on my shoulder
Every step that we take
Is so beautiful in His sight
(Chorus)

All I ask from our Father
When day's end is in sight
is that together forever
We'll walk in His Holy light

My life is made so beautiful
Every smile that you give
May I make your life full
And by your side may I live

(Outro Chorus:)
Oh yeah, I'll kiss you every morning,
And I'll kiss you every night
There's no way I won't be near you
In every day's sweet light

Oh yes I will I will I will I will
Yes I will kiss you every morning
I will kiss you every night
Because you smile in the sunshine
And it pulls back every night

(Bb chord) There is no way I won't be near you...

(arpeggio - Bb C D Eb F Eb F Eb D)

(Eb chord) In every morning's light...

(arpeggio - G A Bb C Bb Ab)

(Bb chord)

– Chris R. Powell

Highland Travel

Written on the event of coincidentally coinciding trips to the British Isles.

Jun 16, 2014

May your trip be relaxing yet fun,
Transformative yet peaceful.
Quiet when it needs to be,
And raucous when it should.

May your writing be informed,
and made easier by this journey,
May your camera come home full
Of memories and inspiration.

I will miss you on your way,
Yet look forward to your return.
Exploring the other side from you,
The Erse Sea between us, blue.

The sun will rise o'er you Scottish
Yet set on Irish land
I look forward to Dublin's selfie,
And wave to you 'cross sea and sand.

May your planes be uneventful,
The rail a pleasant course,
The hostels and the hiking
All leading to Scot's freedom's source.

– Chris R. Powell

An Angel's Song

July 13, 2014 – written as a song

I was walking on the seashore
When out of the blue
An angel wrapped in the mists of time
With hair in golden braid

She smiled and she touched my hand
I felt the legends of a thousand lands
She played a harp with sweet melody
And told stories of

a beautiful angel so easy to love
God's sweet mercy right in front of me
Every time you look my way
my heart is in your hand

We spoke of things that I had never said
We wrote of thoughts I had never read
We played notes, we sang songs
We walked together hand in hand

The day may come when sun may set
My angel of glory so free to fly
Until then will you walk with me?
And take my spirit with you to the sky?

My beautiful angel so easy to love
God's sweet mercy right in front of me
Every time you look my way
my heart is in your hand

A beautiful angel so easy to love
God's sweet mercy right in front of me
Every time you look my way
my heart is in her hands
Every time you look my way
My heart is in your hands.

– Chris R. Powell

LAUGHTER

I had always heard that 'relationships take work.' That hardly sounds like fun. In previous experiences, if I spoke to anyone of serious problems, those problems were dismissed as, "Well, relationships take work."

Imagine, instead, a relationship in which every moment is one of wonder, a source of laughter, an occasion to weave a story—or even a saga! Such was the story of Mr. Brown.

One day, while walking my dog on a larger suburban road, with long stretches of businesses right in the middle of residential areas on either side, I came across a neat, clean pair of brown loafers, the two shoes placed tidily side by side at the bottom of a street sign, as if deliberately set there. It was odd, to say the least.

We immediately concluded these shoes must belong to Mr. Brown. (They were brown, after all; what else *could* his name be!) Not long after, as we took a long hike along the shore of the Mississippi, we found a pair of swimming trunks and a T-shirt hanging on a branch of a tree jutting across the sand. There was no one anywhere nearby. Clearly, it was the elusive Mr. Brown, once again leaving his clothes lying around.

The legend of Mr. Brown grew, as we continued, oddly enough, to come across more clothes in odd places. Mr. Brown was a spy, we concluded, on many and mysterious missions. When we looked at a 'house' for sale in Wisconsin —in truth a traditional Roman Catholic church transformed into a house—the story emerged of Consuela, the secret agent who aided Mr. Brown.

Mr. Brown and Consuela and their evolving story and adventures left us laughing until we cried and Emilie thought we were drunk when we hadn't had a thing.

One night, while dining on the rooftop at Stella's Fish Cafe in Uptown Minneapolis, an amazing thing happened: A blue helicopter landed in the empty lot across the street and four stories below. It lifted off and shortly came back and landed again! This time, a man and a couple of kids jumped out and went to an ambulance waiting on the street. It drove off calmly, no rush, no sirens.

Everyone was plastered to the plastic rails of Stella's, watching this strange sight, the waiters included. Our waiter excitedly told us he'd never seen such a thing. We, of course, knew there was only one man who might account for this strange event!

The legend of Mr. Brown grew. Who was he, that he left his shoes and clothes everywhere, worked with the mysterious Consuela, and now arrived in helicopters in the middle of Minneapolis, to drive away in an ambulance?

And so the song of Mr. Brown was born.

Laughter is vital to love. Life is hard—for everyone. No matter how blessed they might seem on the outside, no matter how rich or beautiful or talented they might be, every single person carries their own personal griefs: an abusive parent, an ill child, chronic health problems, a cheating spouse, sudden loss of a job, being the family scapegoat, or a hundred other things. When two people come together, they each bring the pain of their own past and they will certainly face struggles together.

Laughter is the oil in the engine. Laughter lightens the load. Laughter lets us see the beauty of the world around us, even when we're hurting.

Laughter changes everything, our entire outlook. And when our outlook changes, our life changes. We relate to each other from a much better place if we can laugh at life and see the humor in the world around us.

We become happier and healthier when we laugh and when we laugh together, we are more connected.

I have long said that my life is evidence of God's sense of humor. It never does to take life—or especially ourselves —too seriously! Humor and love are inextricably woven together. A God of love could not be a God without laughter. And in our human relationships, where there is love, there is joy, where there is joy, there is laughter. Where there is laughter, there is joy, and where there is joy, there is love.

– Laura Vosika

Mr. Brown

Sept 2014 – Laughter

Chorus:
Mr. Brown gets around
He gets around town
He gets up, he gets down
Mr. Brown, he gets around

One summer night
The sun still out and bright
A patch of leather
There in the grass
Mr. Brown had been around
Leaving his shoes on the ground
So neatly, right there in the grass
Mr. Brown, where you been?
Where are you now?
Leaving those shoes around town?

(Chorus)

We went down to the river
Maybe to pray the other day
But there in the sand
What's that there? Who's been here?
Mr. Brown, you been here to play?
He done left his shorts here on the shore
With nothin' left to say
But that Mr. Brown done surely been 'round
Hangin' here by the river
On a summer's day

(Chorus)

Downtown at Uptown
On the roof on a Saturday night
Seafood on the top
A helicopter flies over
and lands right in front of a cop!
Pilot gets out, and jumps right on in
To an ambulance there, just waitin'
Off they ran
Mr. Brown, is that you flyin' around?
It didn't look like you had your shoes on
Runnin' to catch that van

(Chorus)

Mr. Brown, please give us the story
What you doin' runnin' all 'round?
Catching you is like catching a song
Like a wig on a heron
We just want to know
When you're up, and when you're down
How are you gettin' around?
With no shorts and no shoes
Flyin' your copter downtown
You give us the blues
Chasing you around, Mr. Brown

(Chorus)

– Chris R.. Powell & Laura Vosika

My Swedish Friend

Jan 18, 2016

Sung to the tune of *My Sweetest Friend*
by the Goo Goo Dolls

Many thanks and love go to our son/step-son and
daughter-in-law for introducing us to this wonderful song
at their wedding.

I'll eat meatballs by the plateful
Princesstarta fills my mouth full
Cover me with lingonberries
I'll come to you on Stena ferries
Keep me warm inside my head
With Svedka Vodka we'll drink in bed
A fortune teller came up to me
Gave me lefse with butter for free
Butter for free…

Come to me my Swedish friend
We'll get lost in Stockholm again
Take me back where I belong
We'll eat lutefisk all night long
Come to me with long blonde hair
This hat from me on your head so fair
And when we're cold again and again
We'll put on all these mittens my friend.

I caught you with that wreath again
Like Santa Lucia is your friend
Flaming hair is not pretty
Those candles should have batteries
We should grab those cookie tins
And strong coffee to make us grin
Anything to ease the strain
Of all that lutefisk, my stomach aflame
Stomach aflame…

Come to me my Swedish friend
We'll get lost in Stockholm again
Take me back where I belong
We'll eat lutefisk all night long
Come to me with long blonde hair
This hat from me on your head so fair
And when we're cold again and again
We'll put on all these mittens my friend.

Today's the day I'll get it this time

Yo-te-bury, not Go-te-borg
Bara bra, tack, I'm fine thank you,
God morgon, Hello, good morning, too

Come to my Swedish friend
Your language is so hard to learn
Word

Come to me my Swedish friend
We'll get lost in Stockholm again
Take me back where I belong
We'll eat lutefisk all night long
Come to me with long blonde hair
This hat from me on your head so fair
And when we're cold again and again
We'll put on all these mittens my friend.

– Chris R. Powell

HUMOR & LOVE

Release. Laughter. Knowing deep within, that you can laugh, so very deeply, so very…shared; that deep, rollicking, rolling, uncontrollable, tears-flowing, raucous, knee-slapping laughter. A shared joke, perhaps that only the two of you get, yet permanently shared between you, and causing so much, so *very* much laughter. You look into each other's eyes, and the tears flow, the bladder practically bursts, you're laughing so hard. It can be over so something so very, well, *silly*, and yet, it is shared, between the two of you.

That is love. It really is. *Love* shares that kind of laughter. Rollicking, rolling, uncontrollable Laughter.

It is a serious root of Love: Pure. Eternal. If you can laugh—at yourself—at yourselves—at everything around you—Literally Everything—it helps. For better or worse. For richer or poorer. For healthier or sicker. *Everything* is going to happen to you. Everything *has* happened to you. You left each other. You got back together. You made fun of each other. You caused the worst, you caused the best. You did the best, you did the worst.

And yet—you're here, you love each other, you will

never leave each other, you're devoted, you're Permanent. You are as intertwined as vines wrapped around each other. A shared sense of humor is like the little suckers on those vines, sticking to the stucco on the ancient building, on the trunk of the tree, on God Himself, sticking to Faith, Hope, and Love.

Surely God laughs as much as He Loves, as much as He Cries for each one of us, as much as He craves each one of us to be near Him and His Son, our Savior. He sees the folly of so much in this world, and He sets up so many practical jokes in our lives as much as He sets up so many beautiful scenes every dear day that He creates. For every tragedy that may befall us—for every awful loss, there are a thousand laughs, a thousand cheers, a thousand beautiful thoughts, sunrises, flowers, and sunsets that are available to us through Him. I am truly convinced of that. And central to that are those belly-laughs that get us through even the darkest of times.

At my maternal grandfather Ralph's funeral, a funeral where I cried deeply, I also laughed heartily, remembering so many practical jokes, belly laughs, and broad, deep smiles that crossed his face every day I knew him. He was one of God's most cheerful people on this Earth. He has governed how I look at life and love for most of my life, especially since I lost my father at a very early age.

I imagine God Himself has that same twinkle in His eye that my GrandDad did—and must still. It is that same twinkle that two people who love each other very much bring to every day, as they wake up next to each other, see each other as their first sight, and realize that good humor, good love, and goodness, will greet them throughout the rest of that day.

Imagine such blessing greeting your days. Do not imagine it—make it happen. It is as close as your next morning.

– Chris R. Powell

Sky Painter

Sept 23, 2014

Nature creates an impression
The Sky Painter makes it her mission
To capture it. There!
Plucked right from thin air.
The beauty, the color, the touch, and the moment,
The figure, the leaf, the ripple, and shadow.
The blue sun shines, and the magenta haze mists,
The heron stands still, and leaves rustle and twist
Roots swim in pond water, and the turtle is captured,
A bee in flight sits, with the viewer enraptured.
A dragonfly buzzes, and summer is set,
The Sky Painter walks, and this image she gets.
I follow her eye, and I'm led to believe,
that I'm there by her side, my arm on her sleeve -
looking intently beyond, through branch,
    flower, and pine,
she treads lightly on Earth, taking winks of sunshine,
this reflection of light, the picture the Father intended,

when He woke us this morning,
    our minds with sleep mended.

Why can't we see, why can't we feel?
What the Sky Painter finds -
Her soul is connected, to this painting projected,
    on sky, sun, and ground, these images found.
We're lucky she sees what others cannot,
    so when she walks on Earth lightly,
    and to life goes her thought,
    her gaze finds the peace, that Nature has wrought;
The deer and the duck, the shine and mist lifted,
Here looking at love, the beauty is sifted.
She brings us a smile, and our lives are made better.
Indeed, Nature was there, on the Sky Painter's journey,
    playing in front of her paintbrush today.
I will be by her side, I will follow her there,
Let me touch what she sees, what she picks from the air,
    let me walk with her there in the sun -
The Sky Painter found my heart's longing and care
    and with it—I want to make one.

– Chris R. Powell

Beautiful Sunday Lady

Jan 13, 2015

My beautiful Sunday lady
Dressed like a heavenly dream
A blessing to my soul,
Love's never-ending stream.

I awoke that night in darkness
The smell of wonder in your hair
Wrapped around you sweetly,
My life in Heaven began right there.

How can I make known to you
The perfection that you are?
That always-present feeling,
Within me, yearning's burning, blazing star.

Your smile will always return me
To that smell of Heaven in your hair
Your crystal blue eyes see through me,
To love's yearning that is there.

My soul will always be open
My life a beautiful song
Every day a new verse written,
Forever building, honest, strong.

To be by you once more today
My arm again joined to your waist
Walking through life together,
Every day may I be graced.

A kiss from lips so beautiful
So soft, yet strong, and sensual
You send me to the sky
Every single kiss is unforgettable

I touch your skin, I feel you quiver
We draw close, almost one together
My joy and life embrace you completely,
Inside and out, in all ways, ending never.

The world is made more beautiful
My Sunday lady by me still
I can't begin to tell you,
My heart's overflowing thrill.

I pray every day and so to deserve
This ray of Heaven's unending light
That flows through you to my soul,
Taking me ever closer to unerring height.

Thank you, my beautiful Sunday lady,
For every moment that we share
I only wish for more such time,
With a life so complete, so fine, so fair.

– Chris R. Powell

Thoughts on Easter Vigil

April 4, 2015, Easter

Shortly after we met, Chris asked to attend Mass with me. I was skeptical about his reasons for wanting to join me. He was a Baptist. It happened that Kim, a Lutheran friend of mine from college, was in town the same weekend, so the Baptist, the Lutheran, and the Catholic all went to Mass together. Sounds like the beginning of a joke, doesn't it!

After Mass, I greeted Father Connelly (to this day, one of my favorite priests) and jokingly told him I was reeling in a couple more. Kim and Chris both *vehemently* shook their heads *No!*

But funny things happen on the way to the forum.

By September, Chris started RCIA—the Rite of Christian Initiation for Adults. I was his sponsor throughout the next months as he attended weekly classes to learn what the Catholic faith teaches.

Catechumens are welcomed into the Church on Easter Sunday. Shortly before, they attend a retreat. Their sponsors are asked to write them a letter talking about their faith journey. I wrote mine in the form of a poem.

Years later, I found that he had saved it, carefully folded in a drawer, during those in-between years.

Not so long ago—less than a year before
You'd never stepped inside a Catholic door
Are you surprised what's happened so fast?
Now you're going to daily Mass!

It seems you had faith on your own
A desire to search and study and learn
Yet still, we're finally called to home,
An ancient school more deeply to discern
Where we better, stronger, faster will be
– Like Lee Majors for all eternity!

How has your faith grown in a year, they asked
It's a difficult question for it seems you'd faced
The worst with humor and faith intact

Yet your prayer rose up to a higher place
Perhaps in seeing how little we know,
We leave more room for virtue to grow?

Trusting the Church to teach us the way,
The path of many a great mind and saint,
Giving our lives to God, giving up our say—

It isn't a path for the weak or the faint.
It promises peace, but is not always smooth
It brings us to truth, which does not always soothe

Perhaps this is the growth that I see
From someone who's done things all on his own
To acknowledge with all humility
The smartest among us have things to be shown
A greater wisdom to be sought and learned
A greater holiness not to be spurned

The question was put, how your walk has helped me—
Inspired my faith and made it flourish?
After twenty-five years, is it easy to see
That we still need something to feed and nourish,
That shows our faith matters, that others perceived
The change in our lives, because we believe?

Life brings us trouble. It's easy to wonder
Amidst the messes in each day
Was my faith foolish, just a blunder?
Would it be better to follow the world's way
It affirms my faith, when I see
That others cherish its fruits in me

What do I hope as you step through this door?
Into the most wondrous, eternal adventure
That life has to offer? I wish ever more
That God will paint brightly your life without censure

Of ongoing miracles of the sort you have felt
In moments of surprise as you knelt.

Life is what happens while we make other plans
And God brings the greatest surprises of all
As we loosen our grip and fall into His hands
And trust the narrow gate in the wall
May life become bigger than you ever conceived
As you trust to the path of the Saints who believed.

– Laura Vosika

New Year's Eve

12.31.15

The New Year's Eve I miss the most
Is that when you gave your dearest kiss
The love you saved for me
Gave to me my dearest bliss
Your rarest treasure
In that moment I knew your love
And that of Father, Son, and Holy Ghost.

– Chris R. Powell

Ostinato Oceanus

New Year's Eve 2015-2016

The ocean's ostinato lays the pulsing beat
Its surging surf is rolling, romping at my feet
A seagull's cry, a sharp descant
Sounds against a sapphire sky
And leaping joyfully in between
A child's laughter brings
A bubbling, joyful melody
Skipping above a harmony
Of whispering wind
That blows my hair free

– Laura Vosika

ROMANCE & BUTTERFLIES

faith

Harlequin has been with the world since the 1950s and in the United States since the 1970s. By 2012, pulp romance novels were a 1.5-billion-dollar industry. While their level of graphic sex varies from almost nothing to quite erotic, the stories have in common a thread of what could be called idealism or, on the flip side—unreality.

They are full of tropes. The heroine is smart and sexy with incredibly beautiful hair and usually a pretty good education and job. She is invariably 'feisty,' a strong, independent woman with a mind of her own and quick to call out men on any perceived wrong—not afraid to stand up for herself. The man is a good six feet or more and built with rippling muscles tapering down to a narrow waist. He's smart, accomplished, and often crazy wealthy. He's ridiculously good-looking. He's chosen his name from a select set of 30 or so names suitable for his sort. And together? Well, sparks fly. Even though they hate each other to begin with, their physical reaction to one another cannot be contained. It's explosive! Romance? Off the charts—once they get over their animosity, of course. He can't keep his eyes off of her. Her hair smells amazing.

Most importantly, when she invariably gets angry and stamps her foot (literally or figuratively—and she always does), he never says, "Wow, you've got a bad temper! No wonder you're still single!" No, he's always the more turned on by her 'feistiness.'

Such books can be a relaxing escape, if not taken seriously. But they're churned out by the hundreds every month. Tens of thousands of women devour them, not only living vicariously through these pert, sexy, *feisty* women, always well-endowed and with amazing 'manes' of hair— but also teaching themselves that this is the way people and the world really are.

These unrealistic expectations—of men, relationships, marriage, and life—have become pervasive throughout our society, causing, for all too many, a poor notion of what love should look like. How many believe it's only love if all these things are present, if there are butterflies and explosive emotions and staggering physical reactions as unstoppable as a train?

We may underestimate what we have because we don't feel those wild butterflies or because some element of society's view of 'love' is missing. There may be a hundred wonderful things—laughter, fun, working and creating together, joy. But we've learned the wrong ideas about what love really is.

It's possible to fall prey to these ideas; to think that someone else deserves all that the movies and songs and novels portray; to wish them to find better than what we have to offer, to believe they deserve better than what we ourselves have, that they should have the Whole Romance Package.

Sometimes, we do the wrong thing despite having the right intentions. But life has a way of teaching us lessons about what love really is—about *service* and *forgiveness,* among other things.

Sometimes—we find that maybe we really had more to offer than we believed.

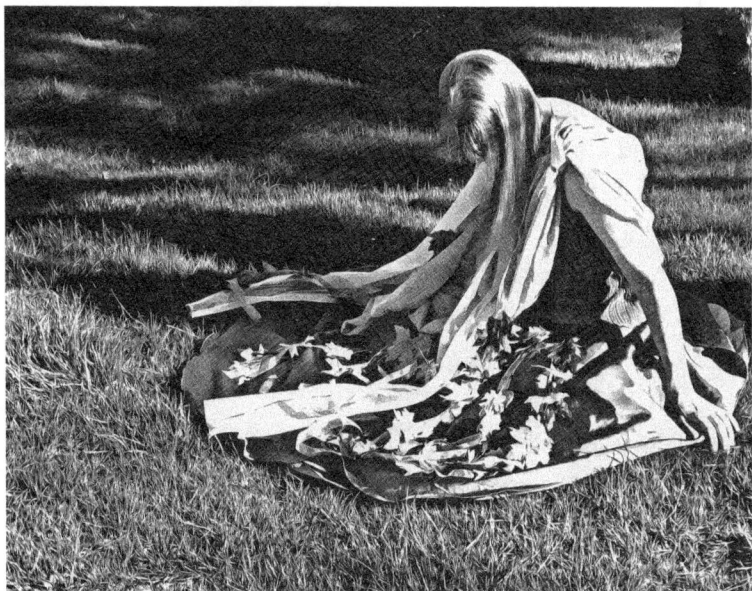

A Hall of Doors

August 14, 2018

I look at a hall with doors and doors
And I can open only one
And through that door I go
    into another hall with doors and doors
And I can open only one
And look back never more to the door
That might have been

And if this hall grows dark
Who am I to complain?
For the door I might have chosen
    in its stead
 May have been been darker still
But then it might have led to light
And yet it's all a roll of dice

And so I stand in this hall with doors and doors
    Counting blessings or cursing fate
And wonder — wonder –
What might have been
As I stand before another door deciding

    – Will I go in?

– Laura Vosika

A DOOR APART

Can You Cry in Her Arms

Can you cry in her arms?
I'd think that would be hard
She only wants one thing from you now
And that's your credit card.
~And the life she's grown to love.

Can you tell her when you're hurt
And living in a fog?
Good luck with that.
She's only married to your job,
~And the life she's grown to love.

You wanted to treat her like a princess,
And now she thinks that's what she's owed.

My dearest love, when you feel alone, know this:
    You have reaped what you have sowed.
    Kiss for kiss, and blow for blow.
    ~You have the life she's grown to love.

Was it your honor that chose her,
    or is your love that true and strong?
You say you're happy, yet I think
    her love for you is long gone.
My dearest love, if somehow I knew,
That she was there and strong for you,
It would give me peace. But I don't think it's true.
    ~I think the life of opulence is what she loves.

– Laura Vosika

WALKING IN FAITH

We're not a world that believes in miracles, says Carol in my *Blue Bells Chronicles,* when she is confronted with a shocking miracle. *Not really.* We pray and we hope—but then we often wonder if an answered prayer was *really* answered prayer from a God who so often feels invisible and silent—or if it was just dumb luck, something that was going to happen anyway.

And then—I wonder how much we *really* want to feel God's presence in our lives. *He's wild, you know. Not a tame lion,* Mr. Tumnus says to Lucy in *The Lion, the Witch, and the Wardrobe.* More to the point, Mr. Beaver tells her: "'Course he isn't safe."

There is something *safe* about keeping God at a distance, about saying we want Him in our lives, and definitely wanting His blessings, but keeping God Himself invisible and silent. There is something frightening, even terrifying, in thinking: the Creator of the Universe, He who holds the world and life in His hands—has taken a very personal interest in *me*?

What if He expects something of me? Wants me to stop doing something I like doing? Change my life? What if He tells me to go to Nineveh, as he did Jonah? What if His plan for my life isn't *my* plan for my life? It's much easier to ignore those uncomfortable expectations and restrictions if we keep Him silent and invisible—if we just toss out prayers now and again and hope He'll give us what we asked for, like an ATM, without actually tapping us on the shoulder.

But God is a very personal God. He *is* involved in our lives. He sees each of us and loves each of us as if we are the only one He has to think about. He does have plans and expectations for the life He has given us. And He takes a very personal interest. He's not tame, they tell Lucy—but he is *good*.

When Isaac, in the Bible, came of age, his father Abraham sent his most trustworthy servant on a journey: Find a wife for my son, from a good family. The servant reached the town of Nahor and there, prayed at a well. "Lord, make me successful today. I am standing beside this spring. May it be that when I say to a young woman, 'please let down your jar that I may have a drink,' and she says, 'Drink, and I'll water your camels, too,' — let her be the one you have chosen.' It happened as he asked. Rebekah offered to water his camels, too. She married Isaac—a union which led to the fulfillment of God's covenant with Abraham.

One writer uses this story—and others from the Bible— to say that God is a God of love—and also of romance. While perhaps none of us have the grand destiny of Rebekah and Isaac, I believe God has never stopped taking such a personal interest in our lives *and in our relationships.* He has a plan and a future for us, Jeremiah tells us. Paul, in his letter to the Romans, promises them (and us) that all things work together for *good,* for those who love God. Dr Mary Neal tells, in her story of her death experience, of coming to the powerful understanding, in her time in Heaven, of how every single thing that happens in our lives, no matter how dark it seems, really *does* give us something God wants for us.

He has a plan. If we dare open our eyes, if we sincerely ask for *God's* will, we may find God interceding in our relationships in shocking ways, working miracles to bring us to where He wants us—and with whom.

It is shocking to suddenly see Aslan, with his giant mane and jaws bigger than your face, nose to nose with you. He is not *safe.* It humbles as it forces us to ask what we've *really* believed all this time.

But if we let Him—and often enough even if we don't—God will stun us with the ways He reveals Himself.

– Laura Vosika

Emmanuel's Light

Twelfth of April

You're leaving tomorrow and this I know
Congratulations, a celebration!
In sultry southern destination,
    while I to the west will go

Our paths have parted and splayed apart
So why this Presence in head and space and heart
More real than the feel of the boy beside me?
For miracles happen when least expected
The words are strong, a clear decree:
We're still connected,
What we've torn asunder shall be corrected
You're leaving tomorrow, yet a promise is made
Wishful thinking? A mind's charade?
What's promised cannot come to pass
You've chosen another path
I will not interfere –
    And yet—the words are clear:
        Just wait—he will be here.

– Laura Vosika

April Promise

An April day, a promise made
A miracle in the April sun
Is it for this I prayed?
An April day, a promise made
The silent words that bade
Me trust Your work's not done
An April day, a promise made
A miracle in the April sun

– Laura Vosika

Come Build Sand Castles with Me

She comes to you with poem in hand,
Whispers of making love to you,
A marble god in gray-veined hue
She comes to you from your own dark land
Holding out her scarlet hand
On forest floor, her clothing strewed
Her sultry promise a toxic brew
She has your hopeful heart in hand
While I build castles in the sand
Knowing no man is a marble god
Watching you drugged by loveless bliss
Descend into her Harlequin land
Knowing the life you live is a fraud

   – But it's my castles you'll finally miss

– Laura Vosika

The Cat Twists Slowly

May 9, 2018

The cat twists slowly around my ankles
    As I walk
Slowly, in and out between my feet
    Tripping me, sliding in front of me
    Behind me, around me
So carefully I step, tremulous
    Fearing a fall

I push him away
    And he is back, undaunted
    Unswayed

I sit, and he is there
    On my lap, on my wrists
    climbing, paws on shoulders
    Paws at my hair
    Pushing his nose to my cheek

His nose in my ear
      Tickling my neck with his
            pink sandpaper tongue

I push him away—
      I have work to do!
      And he is back, undaunted
      Unswayed

And this cat has a name
It is named
      Thoughts of You

I crawl into sleep and he is
      Under the bed, rustling, meowing
      Scratching at something
      Purring happily
      And now he's in bed beside me

Thoughts of You will not leave me alone
      Curled on my stomach
      On my shoulder
      Pinning me down

I've given up trying to push him away

– Laura Vosika

Silent God

July 1, 2018

How silent is my God
With nothing more to say
His voice has waned away

How silent, God,
how quiet you've become
I strain to hear your voice
You are not to be heard

– Laura Vosika

A Vision of the Afterlife

January 2017

What harsh division rankled here on earth
And drove us far apart
What misunderstandings and pride and wrongs
Eating at our hearts

Your fingers slipped from mine
Once loving to the touch
You stormed away with wounded pride
And icy accusations and angry words and such

But in my rest I see a summer day
Where love melts hearts once cold with pride
Your hands reach out, your eyes light up
Into love and light we walk
All wounds and anger cast aside

– Laura Vosika

Just Over the Sunset

2017

I can see you just over the sunset
I can feel you even though you are gone
Why is there such a deep hole inside me?
So many smiles, yet now I'm alone

In the wind we shake hands as friend
The warmth of a smile no one can forget
All our closeness we all take for granted
Where are you now? It seems like we just met

I can see you just over the sunset
I can feel you even though you are gone
Why is there such a deep hole inside me?
So many smiles, yet now I'm alone

In this world we're all lucky
If we find a friend close enough to share
Pass through life only once as a family
A quilt of life sewn together with care

I can see you just over the sunset
I can feel you even though you are gone
Why is there such a deep hole inside me?
So many smiles, yet now I'm alone

I've come to think my life just gets better
With every friendship, my life-quilt grows
        easier to bear
Even though you're now in my memory
I'll smile forever, you'll always be there

I can see you just over the sunset
I can feel you even though you are gone
Why is there such a deep hole inside me?
So many smiles, yet now I'm alone

– Chris R. Powell

Hemlock's Lace

December 10, 2017

There's a pain that never goes
It's rooted deep within
And it stings anew
Each time you ignore me again

There's a pain that grows
Of hemlock's blooming lace
Of thrashing stormy waves
Each time you turn your face

A pain so soft, no one knows
Of its nettles in my skin
For I hide your name
And hope for joy again

– Laura Vosika

Another Year Past

January 1, 2017

The road that we have traveled
The stories our lives have writ
The lasting friendships and
Broken loves our hearts have fit
In spaces that were pure and whole

Told in another year that has reached its dusk
In another year flown by
And still the gulf remains my love
Separating you and I

Another year has faded away
Into its dusky past
But no amount of passing time
Can sever our ties at last

– Laura Vosika

Aster Cafe Triolet

February 27, 2020

It was a cold March day
the snow lay late that year and deep
When first we met at the Aster Cafe
On a cold and windy March day
I return alone and ask what we let slip away
As I watch the Earl Gray slowly steep
Pondering that cold winter day
When the snow lay late and deep

– Laura Vosika

I Found Myself Alone

November 12, 2020

I found myself alone
And I sought out love
Oh how I searched
and yet when I
found love, I failed to recognize
it; I failed to see that
I had found it; a

Need so deep
A need so strong
It was need for things I
hardly knew I needed; you
filled that need and
Your need—
Need I fill
You with such love
Fill you with hope; may
I give you new joy
Let me bring you new life as

Much as you have filled me
As you have given me joy
You fill me

    I

           Need

              You

– Chris R. Powell

Chimney Sweeps

December 8, 2019

Somewhere in London under a smoke-filled sky
The sweeps are dancing on the gables
   under the sooty stars
And somewhere in London,
   far below their chimney stacks
Annabelle stretches, a languid lioness
While beside her David sleeps

She stares at the ceiling and thinks of James
Oh James! The wisest fool and saddest man
He chose a queen he hadn't seen!
And wooed her from her Danish Marsh

To the window Annabelle glides
To watch the smoky, starry skies
While David sleeps
And the buildings rise

Blotting out the countryside
    And somewhere out there she sees
        – As if through the walls
        – And down the marble halls

    James lies awake in his golden bed
    His queen in white asleep at his side
    But now he's seen and now he knows
    What she tried to hide
        Beneath a cross of gold
    On moonlit nights,
    He's now been told,
    It swings as she sways
        Through the dark alleyways
        And past the opium dens
    Up to the rooftops and smoky stacks
        With white gown and gold cross
        She dances with sweeps in sooty black

    Foolish wise James to the window goes
    Thinking of spring with Annabelle
    Crying prayers he'll never tell
    As he scans the sooty streets
    His queen is dreaming of chimney sweeps
    All while David blissfully sleeps

    – Laura Vosika

To Be a Mote of Dust

Oh to be a mote of dust in a ray of sun
A wisp, a twist, a breeze, a quisp
   alight this feather on my heart
I see a mote of dust herein
   in this arid, barren day
I cast my vision alight upon the sky
Heavenward an angel bends toward
   silkenward, waterward, flowing, ebbingward, so
   I can't see it, her? She is there I know
The content of this cloud
   There is none here, ramp, sky, ground, fly high
Flying now with wings not mine
   I cannot both see and comprehend
This winged, aloft, this singed, Icarus bent
   How can I be blessed, know?
A feather tossed upon an angel's breath
It seems to have its journey, sent
God, indeed, mysterious now, yet always
   in control, so He must ever onward go
To tell the others at the service where

I must pray under my breath doth
The sun breaks over, the dew is gone, to know
A frog leaps now, fly in arc, rain drop, fall
Ant with leaf, mayfly born, this way he goes,
    gone night, gone
Time flows, yet? Or maybe not, how can we know?
None here do, this, Inward bliss,
    Onward, go, just, go, or, no?

I study, I read, I try to "get"
    It is one that is wrong, I'm not the song
I sit outward here, to chart this path
A goner, a loner, most wrong, most long

Remember the mote? Here I dote,
    Here I sit
Lift up my thought, lift up my sight
Heavenward, Skyward, Beyond my...self.

Escape this...stuff...and...

    Fly...so

        High

– Chris R. Powell

Mirror

February 16, 2020

Once I held before my face
A mirror crafted by the world
And in it, oh, how full of grace
Did I appear

I failed to see the mirror's cracks and sooty stains
Reflecting the world's contorted view
Too entranced with who stared back

Then came Christ to make it shine
A mirror forged by God Himself
I hardly knew the face was mine
So dark did it appear

– Laura Vosika

FORGIVENESS

Love keeps no record of wrongs, Corinthians tells us.

There are plenty of relationships where one person is largely at fault—cheating, stealing, abusing or more. But it's likely more common that both people have made their mistakes. Love shines through when each is quick to admit their own fault and apologize and equally quick to forgive.

There are thousands of articles written on forgiveness. Pastors tell us it is good for our soul; doctors tell us it is good for our physical health; psychologists and religious leaders tell us *how* to forgive, sometimes in lengthy articles and with detailed steps.

But the truth is—I wonder if anyone can really give step by step instructions for how to forgive. I've made a conscious study of the topic of forgiveness since I was in high school. One conclusion I've reached is that true, deep, genuine forgiveness comes, not from what we *do,* but from who we *are*. It comes from humility and love.

The more humility we have, the more clearly we see our own faults. The more we recognize our own fallibility, the easier it is to forgive the faults of another.

The more we have love in our hearts—the *agape* love for all mankind—the more naturally forgiveness flows. When we begin to see other people as children of God, deeply loved by Him, as people God wants in His arms; when we begin to see others come, like us, to God, to others, and to the world, in all their brokenness—then we begin to understand that the ugliness men put into the world comes from the pain and brokenness they feel inside.

Hurting people hurt people.

We are all victims of *victims.*

When we begin to see others—even the worst—as hurt and broken children, and when we have the humility to see our own shortcomings, forgiveness is suddenly no longer something we *try for*. It's something that begins to happen on its own—because we first loved.

When two people come to each other with love and humility, forgiveness flows on both sides. Things that could have left us angry fade into the past or are even laughed about.

Love brings forgiveness and forgiveness brings greater love.

– Laura Vosika

Broken Bones

February 16, 2020

How do I ask forgiveness
For the broken bones that were me?
You met me and saw beauty
You missed the broken bones
  You didn't see

I forgive the scars and wounds
That were you
You were battered and broken too
And both of us smiling in our fine garb
Our shimmering silver robes
Of intellect and wit
That covered the wounds and scars

But perhaps I am more guilty
For I judged your tilted gait
While you saw only beauty in mine.

I ask forgiveness for the
Broken bones that were me.
I ask forgiveness for my failure to see

– Laura Vosika

Days of Our Acquaintance

February 16, 2020

I've long believed that a good love poem or song is one that might equally be spoken to God.

I have reviewed the days of our acquaintance
Starting with the first rush of recognition
Excitement of a kindred soul
Of a mind quick and curious and alive

I have reviewed the days of our acquaintance
Your flaws and failures – and mine
That clouded a sun begging to shine
I scrambled back from your persistent love
Your blind relentless pursuit
And failed to recognize my own faults –
   – In the days of our acquaintance

– Laura Vosika

Forgive Me the Times

Forgive me. The times I failed you
Were hardly my fault. Why must you
Be so harsh? So critical and
Condemning, so full of anger?

But still, I ask, will you ever
Forgive me those times? I failed you,
It's true. I could have tried harder
Been more patient, waited longer

Held my tongue and my own anger
Maybe...I need to ask you...to
Forgive me the times I failed you.
Will you ever see and believe

The depths with which I loved you true?
I wish I had never hurt you
I plead, I hope, I pray that you
Forgive me the times I failed you.

– Laura Vosika

Love to Shame

January 2021

The cross I have carried has cut deep and hard,
each step down this road, each splinter, each shard-
The shoveler dug deeper into me still,
But beyond it there was more tragedy still,
I looked to transcend St. Peter's book's quill,
       another cross thrust upon these shoulders strong,
       another journey, with many steps long.

Mixed faith and folly with faithlessness, tossed,
My spirit, my heart, my soul, nearly lost,
And worse, my precious creation, my heart,
This one so tiny on entry to this mortal part,
Emotionally burned and needlessly singed,
Each day's simple things, with such venom, tinged.

This cross I found firmly planted and ground,
Leaden and greasy, with cords round me wound,

It pulled me and dragged me in all sorts of ways,
Determining where to go—impossible most days,
Identity slipping, tracking wants and needs,
Mortgaged myself towards Self-Obsessed's needs,
Each seed sowed and planted, each vine a new weed,
Each weed a new cord wound round the cross a new lead,
Each lead a new direction pulling this way and that,
'Til that cross would fall over, pounding me flat,
Rise up each day, to fall and fail again,
As new seeds, weeds, and leads,
        told me I'm wrong there and then.

Where does one's soul go on a journey like that?
Via Dolorosa? Golgotha, perhaps?
To revisit salvation, at least, some purposeful way?
No. This journey was baseless and senseless
        and needless and yet,
Endless and looping with new ways to "got get."

It started one day, sweetly enough,
as such things do, with shared interests and stuff,
A smile, and some sun, a walk hand-in-hand,
Amazingly enough, we like the same band-
Coincidences abound, a shared faith at the top,
Without this number one, this'd have to stop.

Marriage is important: She'd never been,
I needed one, to book-end perfection.
Things went along, progressing "just fine?"

Shamans, and pagans, along for the ride
My faith took a back seat, lip service it got
Nary a Mass or Confession, or Rosary begat
After moving together, starts the inevitable slide
The picking, the nits, the tatting, the clips
Every day there was something, caused her mood to flip
The nearing, the fearing, the hiding, the stress,
Just avoid, move away, get away from this mess
Some days wrecked on rocks within moments of starting,
Some took more hours before finding monsters hiding

Every day insides churning awaiting the shoveler,
I knew he was coming to take what's inside me
Nothing was good enough,
       "must be nice" if I tried
       to take some time off on my own,
        especially outside
       "Don't do that", "you're a putterer,"
       "these books are a mess",
All these problems I had, I just had to confess,
After a while, it just becomes easier to withdraw,
    from
      everything
        that makes me
          What and Who
            I …
                was, because I've

forgotten these things

since it's easier to cope by giving them wings-
and digging myself a deeper hole down,
To try to escape this self-obsessed hound,
hounding, and pounding, and trouncing my sense,
of self and my head, and my heart, and my spirit,
the farther I go, the less I can hear it.

I came near to soul's end in this endless despair,
As I sought refuge in a box with a lid and no care,
I tried nailing it shut from everyone outside,
Figuring, I'm done now, nothing's left, not even my pride,
I'd always been jolly and full of good cheer,
I'd always found humor; oft raised a beer,
But this cross had no noble purpose, and no noble end,
All the weeds had wrapped 'round me,

     the hard parts hammered in,

   My energy was sapped, I was empty and lonely,

    I was done,

       and done,

       and....

        Done...

– Chris R. Powell

An Angel Shall Forge, a Child Shall Lead

July 17, 2018

Written on a vision

The forest grew, like fairy tale briers
Of thick, enclosing thorny vice
And the leaves so thick above,
The sun no longer touched the ground

And deep in this shadowed forest, a man alone
In clothes of web and soot
Surrounded by thorns
He strained to see the light
As the tangled vines grew closer still

And lifted his voice in one sad cry

And then before him stands a man of light
Of shoulders broad and towering height
A sword of flames at his side

The sword swings high, the sword swings wide
Slicing back the thorns
And underneath—a cobbled path of gold

And slowly, longer, grows the path
A narrow lonely sentinel between
    the pressing vines

The man in soot hesitates
He knows the demons that wait
To reach from the forest and grasp
The unwary, even on this path

He knows the demons by name
For he invited them in
They shriek his name
And name his sins

A child appears with golden hair
Stretching out her hand
Beneath her feet, the path grows bright
With cobblestones of gold

And still he waits

She speaks; her voice is light
"Be fearless, now. Be bold!"

She turns and goes in confidence
Down this path that shimmers with gold

And the black and clawed talons that reach
   from the dark and tangled vines
Fall back
   – afraid

He hastens behind
And as he goes
The soot and dust
   fall from his clothes

Music rises from her feet
The shrieks of the demons wane
The thorns fall slowly back
And the narrow path grows broad

Far ahead, the sword of flame
Flashes and slashes
Again and again

An angel conquers
But a child leads

– Laura Vosika

Hawk

Tell me the truth—for I can't believe
What I see and feel and hear
    for miracles only happen to others

I fling out a fleece of deer and hawk –
A deer for fool, a bird if not

And there sits the hawk atop a post
    jolting me to my core
Yet still I doubt
The fleece I asked for—I ignore

God, how do You not despair
Of us down here on Earth?
Do You roll Your eyes and ask why bother
To intervene in their affair
    to answer all their prayer?

No, I think You view our foibles with mirth
And give back joke for joke
You bided Your time, then once again –

   – You spoke!

A hawk arose!
Erupted from magician's wand!
Hovered before my creeping car
In its talons, drooping frond
Three feet before my startled eyes!
   Surprise!

I felt You chuckle
As it hung suspended
Each tattered feather in sharp relief
It's wings extended
Sweeping away my disbelief

A deer if fool, a hawk if not
Miracles come when least expected
I heard You chuckle and ask...

   Now do you believe?

– Laura Vosika

HOPE

Carillon Bells

February 2, 2020

Under the veil of the carillon bells
Incense rises and holiness swells
Within the hearts of those who kneel
And pray to the great bells' peal

Sing holy, holy, holy the angels cry

– Laura Vosika

Rejoicing I Go

February 6, 2020

With rejoicing I go
To meet my King
Solemnly arrayed in
What little splendor have I

It is little but Oh my King
Is gracious and kind
And looks on me with love
He sees my heart and it is the gold
That edges my poor dress
To make it fit to wear before a king.

Rejoicing I go before my Lord
Who in His goodness summons me
Rejoicing I go, rejoicing I sing
He has summoned me
The Lord of all the land

– Laura Vosika

By the Sea by the Surf

February 16, 2020

By the sea, by the roaring surf
You gave me joy
You gave me sunrise and laughter

By the sea, by the roaring surf
  by pulsing waves
You gave me all I could have wanted
And still I failed to see
That this was love

Immerse me now in waves of compassion
For all our faults and flaws
Immerse yourself in a tender love
Of a heart that needed time to heal
Sink in waves of revelry
For all the joy to come
For soon we will dance on bright hot sand
Beneath a bright and shining Son

– Laura Vosika

RECONCILIATION

A Psalm of Winged Transcendence and Hope

November 10, 2020

A Prayer of Rescue and Thanksgiving

Torn from my heart, and yet I tore
Sent from you, LORD, of all truth and hope
    The road seemed long, yea, longer still
    Yet shorter the path to love did I seek

    The value taught through Word and Wisdom
        is patience first through life's travail
    A Yoke that is given to us light,
    A Savior that is a Gate and Lamb.

    I turned away from an Angel's guide pure
        to stay the course to God's white light
    I thought I could see a shorter path
        to love's necessary place by my side.

Alas, but not, this was not true—
Vex and darkness followed me,
While plying a troth away from truth
I was led to gnashing ruin.

As angel's do, she never left,
        but confused and hurt, she was bereft
In a thin place, a hawk flown
        from God's side did start
the healing needed to build love's heart.

This harbinger from Heaven's place
        wove threads across both time and space,
The loom showed a fabric of many parts,
A ministry and mission to touch many hearts.

The hawk's threads reached me in mysterious ways
A call to play, a call to pray, a dream, a photo diary-
Looking east to sun's rise daily
Sitting in a sanctuary, a rejected library

Although in a sacrament's bond,
I had entered into it clearly wronged
The more this angel's hawk brought threads
The more judgment must rend what was badly wed.

What this loom's comb had finally started,
And what my choices at first had discarded,
My angel now came forth in brightness,
With Raphel in healing and Uriel in lightness

Reaching into my soul in softness,
      what had become so pushed down and darkened,
Was now borne up by eagles wings and harkened
      to Heaven and Angel asking jointly as One
If I would leave behind what I had done—

An Eagle girded me to slake my thirst
for God's Holy blessing to shed this curse-
I reached up to Angel and took her hand,
The fabric of our mission growing as Eagle's wings fanned.

Security, Peace, and Creativity follow,
A swan family glides o'er as we walk through the hollow,
A misty tableau on bended knee
We thank God in Heaven for all He did see.

A fabric that, if made years ago,
      if left to two people could not be as so,
But if left to God's Wisdom and two people's prayers
      and humility, yes, and occasional errors,

When back over time we now look,
Messengers and helpers were in every nook,
the Hawk, and Eagle, and Visions, and Dreams,
Showed us that nothing in life is what it seems.

And now that that Heavenly fabric is ready,
Our Swans demonstrate that we are rock steady-
We look back again and wonder aloud,
        if it could have been different somehow,

But, God, we know, to You be the Glory,
We are so thankful for the rest of our Story.

Amen.

– Chris R. Powell

Love as Sacrament

Love is intended in the Catholic faith to be rationalized as marriage in a sacrament. In a letter to Polycarp, Ignatius of Antioch writes: "It is right for men and women who marry to make their union with the consent of the bishop, that their marriage may be for the Lord and not for passion. Let all things be done for the honor of God." The fourth-century pope Siricus I dictates that the bride be veiled, and Ambrose refers to the "giving away" of the bride. Neither of these customs was taken up in the Christian East, which saw the introduction, instead, of another distinctive tradition: the crowning of both bride and groom with jewels or flowers. The crowns themselves may have been a remnant of Jewish practice (Song of Songs 3:11) or an emulation of Saint Paul's concept of athletic discipline in Christian life (1 Corinthians 9:24–25), or both. John Chrysostom describes crowns as "symbols of victory" over the passions, which suggests an interpretation of the custom that is still popular today: the marriage crown is, in part, a martyr's crown—a reminder of the ascetic dimension of marriage.

These developments reflect a growing esteem for marriage in the early church. Even among those who favored monasticism, there was a strong sense that, when spouses dedicate themselves to each other's sanctification, marriage is a worthy relationship. John Chrysostom, who began his preaching career with a strong animus against marriage, observed, "There is no relationship between people so close as that between man and wife, if they be joined together as they should be."

In a sacramental marriage, God's love becomes present to the spouses in their total union and also flows through them to their family and community. By their permanent, faithful and exclusive giving to each other, symbolized in sexual intercourse, the couple reveals something of God's unconditional love.

The sacrament of Christian marriage involves their entire life as they journey together through the ups and downs of marriage and life and become more able to give to and receive from each other. Their life becomes sacramental to the extent that the couple cooperates with God's action in their life and sees themselves as living "in Christ" and Christ living and acting in their relationship, attitudes and actions.

Catholic teaching holds that sacraments bring grace to those who receive them with the proper disposition. Grace is a way of describing how God shares the divine life with us and gives us the help we need to live as followers of Christ. In marriage, the grace of this sacrament brings to the spouses the particular help they need to be faithful and to be good parents. It also helps a couple to serve others beyond their immediate family and to show the community that a loving and lasting marriage is both desirable and possible.

Pope Paul VI wrote: "By it [the Sacrament of Matrimony] husband and wife are strengthened and... consecrated for the faithful accomplishment of their proper duties, for the carrying out of their proper vocation even to perfection, and the Christian witness which is proper to them before the whole world" (Humanae Vitae, n. 25).

– Chris R. Powell

Cuisle Mo Cridhe

Sept 10, 2020

The day breaks sweet, the sundew, heat,
The godwit wades, the sea retreats.
The Irish grass waves as the breeze blows by,
a brown crab sidles as tides beckon and sigh.

Off the coast of Connemara, the water that is there,
has the bluest-gorm green-glas-glow,
that takes me to the eyes of my bean álainn, Laura fair.
My cushlamachree lady free,
my cailín damhsa dancing girl,
Playing music for my soul,
       strumming heart strings,
       twirls again,

Hair of spun-gold flaxen,
       fresh from Heaven's angel looms,
Godwit, grass, and surf, all bow and wave
       to cailín damhsa as she goes dancing past.
Surely as the sun every day rises in the east,

over my farm and hearth
so humble on this Connemara coast –
one day I shall be worthy
to rise above my common station,
and plight my troth to bean álainn
with her gorm-glas eyes so fair -

We shall marry on the mornin'
     in white and black with horses near:
With lily of the valley, and peony, and rose,
For her sweetness, me for honor,
     and rose for passion, carried three –
With a shamrock for good luck,
     o'course, a-'prayin', a' the way.

The day grows long, the moondew, cool,
     the e'en tide ebbs, the fog rolls in.
The long-eared owl within the copse
     hoots softly low, a muffled chant.
Closely bound and closely found,
     we, together, I and she,
     this e'en fair and e'en thick and e'en dense
     and moon-fair be.
One thing I know, among all else, my tell-tale heart
     that does beat free-
My life complete, my love so sweet,
     my lady free, cushlamachree.

– Chris R. Powell

SERVICE

While statistics can be played with, many studies suggest that arranged marriages tend to fare better in terms of divorce rates than our western model of dating, romance, living together, and choosing our own spouses.

Why?

I believe (and studies also say) it's because these couples look at the components of what makes a healthy marriage, rather than expecting love to happen and magically remain. In fact, there are many, many stories of couples meeting for the first time on their wedding day and finding that love grows.

I believe one of the fundamental components of love is service. Giving to the other. I've seen many people online speak of 'getting their needs met' by their boyfriend/girlfriend or spouse. But it's like the story of the two groups of people sitting around circular tables laden with a feast. Each of these people had only a fork far too long to maneuver into their own mouths. At one table, they refused to help one another—so everyone continued to be hungry and miserable. At the other, they simply stretched out their forks to feed each other—and there was happiness and laughter.

This, to me, is an aspect of marriage. Romance and butterflies come and go. They may fade with time or be tested in times of job loss or family problems or the death of a child. They may be tested when a newer, prettier flower appears on the horizon to excite those butterflies. And if we base our ideas of love on those emotions—well, our feelings can always be excited by someone else. And the truth is— those butterflies, a pretty face, a hot body, steamy sex—can blind us to the things we should really be looking at: character, honesty, integrity, generosity in time and attitude, forgiveness, letting the little things slide—and realizing most things *are* little things. Is your prospective spouse negative or positive? Do they complain endlessly? Do they insist on having everything their way? It's easy to miss or dismiss these things as unimportant, when blinded by butterflies.

I learned this lesson in seeing firsthand that those who profess 'love' do not always fulfill the other ideals I thought were an obvious part of love: putting another first, service, help, loving all that makes that person who they are.

I saw that service and giving *don't* always follow 'love.' I watched a one-way street emerging, of a person who was not there to give to another—but to *get*.

I realized how much I myself had bought into the foolish notion of romance and butterflies and had foolishly assumed service and giving would naturally follow from butterflies.

In fact, the older I get, I suspect it's the other way

around. Often, butterflies follow from giving and service. Love is patient, the Bible tells us. Love is kind. It is not easily angered. *It is not self-seeking.* It does not keep a record of wrongs. *It does not dishonor the other.* It protects.

Perhaps the emotion of love, in truth, more often follows from acts of love—from *service*—which only come from a genuine concern and caring for the well-being of another, rather than from seeking only and always to have 'love' fulfill your own desires.

Real love is about mutually seeking the joy, happiness, and well-being of the other.

– Laura Vosika

So Delicious Thinking of You

Sept 16, 2020

It is so delicious thinking of you...
so completely top-to-bottom, inside-out,
finger-to-toe delicious, just...
thinking of you...

the air tonight has turned cool,
misty-dewy-cool,
and draws me across the fens and moors up to you,

where my lips cannot but warmly
cut through the cool-dew-mist
to join with yours in heat and light and glow

to turn back the drip-dew-hanging-low in the valley,
the fog-puff from your breath parts

and my tongue fashes-dashes-tashes in,
touching your perfect teeth,
resting but for a moment there

as I probe more deeply,
the fog returns

but the heat from my breast rises and
smites the fen-brew gone

as intensity rises...rises...rises...

my touch of your breast causes your breath
to step-stop-stip,
bit by bit,
as you bite my probing-proving-prowling tongue
that continues its journey as my hands do the same...

God I love how you INSPIRE-FIRE ME...
my JOY...
my HAPPINESS returns...in glory...

   ...tingle-fingle-vingle indeed!!!

– Chris R. Powell

On Cuisle's Eve

Sept 23, 2020

As a rain shower washes gently over the soul,
      touching every nerve like a caress,
Leaving behind a tiny wetness,
Like a dewy morning, the fog steals in, on a roll –

My love envelops thee, mo Cuisle, completely,
The combination of that tiny dropness-feel,
With the breeze of summer under a blue sky, real,
Wrapped around you less discretely…

There comes a time when standing upward,
      for what's mine and thine around us, family,
      builds a foundation so firm and mightily,
Seeking, reaching, to our LORD most skyward,

My blessings come in prayers answered,
      our loving's bounty, kisses shared,
A gentle touch like that rain-drop spared,
      suffusing every breath, a tingle, lowered-

This Eve of Cuisle, warm and thoughtful,
        her advent on this world draws nigh,
        celebrating the truth of a love-borne sigh,
A candle lit, it's flame so beautiful-

I reach out for her, and the moon shines
        its starry-eyed vision down,
Blinking through that drop-dew mist,
Our love from the Earth and God,
        forever kiss-twist,
Happy Birthday, I whisper,
        Mo Cuisle, my crown.

– Chris R. Powell

A Warm November Day on Little Butternut Lake

November 10, 2020

A canoe takes light on the placid lake
The cool mists reluctantly find crannies
    among dry catkins and reeds
As the sun finds the crest of an elegant swan,
    who bends down, a drink to take
Sun, ever lower now, colder winds hasten cob's speed
Looking up and back, his mate, his pen, never to forsake.

Swan's bugles play an early morning's reveille-
A late-season cygnet between them
    not yet in full white-satin glory
The early ice still hugs the shore tightly
As the beautiful swans tell their charge
    their lore and family story.

A breeze blows redolent, warm notes of late fall,
as the Indian Summer blazes in full display
Azure sky, crystal waters, grey trees,

even pumpkins floating water-tall,
A geese convention gathers to debate
exactly when to disembark this idyllic way.

The lowered sun begins its departure much too soon,
Our canoe points towards shore
across glossy-glassy water
The camp fire licks and beckons under a rising moon
As our cygnet gently bugles one last query to cob-father.

– Chris R. Powell

I to you am One

Nov 12, 2020

I to you am
One—I, bound with
Your Heart; I, God,
In prayer, you & I
Yet called, I back
To serve, I: you,
Willing, I, to you
I, your heart forever

Love my day starts
To love my day goes
In brightness love gives
All I have is love
She gives love back,
My love to me
Love in my heart resides

You are my sweetest
And you give much
To me. You are
God's gift, yet you
Do all; you are
All, you, to all
You are love indeed.

I

Love

You

– Chris R. Powell

Mo Cuisle Let Me Lift

Nov 12, 2020

Mo Cuisle let me lift
Let me lift you up
Let me lift you up, Mo Cuisle
With words of exhortation

I know who you are
Of seeking and of goodness
And I know the fire
Through which you've walked

And always with a smile and laugh
Mo Cuisle how you've lifted
How you've lifted me up
Mo Cuisle how you lifted me
With words of exhortation

Let me now be the same to you
Let my breath of warmth
And love lift you
Lift you up
Mo Cuisle

– Chris R. Powell

I Love

I
Love my
Love, to love
My love, for love,
in love as love unto
Love as love so wrapped
Up in love for you that
I love thinking about how much I
Can write to you, sing to you and
Think on you, pray on you, and just plain
Love you, building, brick by brick,
    every day, inexorably, growing,
In a way, just like these lines, that flow, like streams,
From my heart, never-ending, forevermore,
    to your ocean, filling you up,
Like all Sol's sunbeams flowing,
    like all of Heaven's angels on alabaster wings,

Sent with my love at once to you, today and everyday,
    filling your ocean,

God knows His Creation, its Beauty,
    and His heart aches and longs for it daily,
I know my sacramental angel that way
    and must bless you in faith and love equally.

– Chris R. Powell

As the Snow Falls

November 16, 2020

As the snow falls,
imagine my kisses
and my days with you
accumulating like wonder
like snow, as bright
and lasting, as light
blowing, laughing, reaching you
swirling around you, just
touching your cheeks
kissing you, leaving just
a light touch, and a smile
as the snow falls
so my love is as
perennial

– Chris R. Powell

HONOR

What is honor? Truly? Integrity. It is the value that stands the test of time. That stands every test. It stands the test of attack – both internal and external. When someone is snide, you stand up. When values are threatened, you stand up. It isn't even a question – honor means HONOR. You put your spouse before everyone and anything, certainly before yourself. One's children and spouse are to oneself the most important persons and aspects to life more precious to life than life itself – there is nothing that could be more important than defending them and keeping them safe and sacrosanct, because every aspect to life, including faith, family, love, and decency, are based in their quality and sanctity of life.

If I honor them, I honor myself, but only as a function of them before me. It is very similar to how leaders in the military treat their soldiers – they only eat, or are housed, once those they command eat, or are housed. And, it isn't some fake aspect to command, it is the very heart of command, of being the head of the household. And, this isn't some arbitrary lordship, it is the very heart of faith itself, of how God intends Man to act to his Wife, and to his family. It is as natural as love itself, as nature itself, and as the very definition of the sacrament of marriage between a man and a woman, architected by God at the time He created Woman to be a companion to Man from within his body, commanding him to honor that creation by virtue of Him who created that companion as He commanded Adam to honor all of His creation in dominion over it.

Dominion demands honor among many virtues, including conservation, respect, integrity, trust, loyalty, kindness, and reverence. All of these are at the foundation of honor in sacramental love in a triumvirate with God, man and woman. Honor is a badge that is worn – on the sleeve, on the heart, on the mind, and on the soul. It is the most visible of the virtues, because it is the one most quickly deployed in the event any threat is visible, especially in a society hell-bent on compromising any and every value, no matter how major or minor.

Imagine two cases – one where a spouse is mortally ill, and the healthy spouse does as the vows require, every day, takes care, binds wounds, tends to infinite needs, meets with doctors, remembers all the meds, therapies, and notes, and carries on for the child and spouse, day after day, as the hospital visits mount and the situation grows more dire and bleak. That spouse acts out of love for an ill partner who gives love, gratitude, in return. This is an example of honor in marriage.

Now imagine a similar situation, where the ill spouse milks the other, obtaining all the same benefits, but not honoring the other, nor being part of a true sacrament, but leaning with harsh expectation and excoriation, leaving the spirit desiccated. There is no love here. There is no honor.

Instead, honor is when two are arm-in-arm, when one smiles at the other, when a door is held for the other, a jacket is put on for the other, a compliment is made, when you cannot but help to smile, simply beam, and tell your spouse in public that they make your life beautiful, showing everyone around you without intending to that the entire world revolves around them and that you are the luckiest person that has every walked God's green Earth. When people come up to both of you and tell you how wonderful it looks just to see you arm in arm, smiling at one another.

Honor is as honor does, every moment of one's life. It is the gift that keeps on giving, and not just to each other, but to everyone around us.

– Chris R. Powell

My Oasis

March 10, 2021

The water of life laps at my feet
In pursuit of my heart, it is ever-present
Each spoonful, each mouthful, each cupful sweet
Laps onward, upward, to me, Heaven-sent

I am in the desert, heat like steel, closing inward
I've walked in sand till my heels were red,
Plodding this way, circling back,
     missing once, twice, thrice
Love's path blindly in the sun, sometimes nice,
     sometimes dread

To arrive at this refuge, this wonder of life
Water of love's earnestness, expressing, cooling thirst
Is magic to a soul encumbered, full of strife
Hearts open room, filling nicely 'til feelings burst

The water fills you and yearning, burning love's desire
Softly soothing, expanse made perfect, leaves me blessed
The contrast made manifest, cooling water passion's fire
My hand raises up to meet Oases
        holding kisses and love's fast

My wife most honest, loving, fetching beauty, Oasis edge
Descended Heaven's stair, pledged her honor,
        faith's clear test
For me the honor, Oasis lapping water's
I respond with vows, full of meaning, blessings blest

Every day, water's soothing, moving, love in purity heart's
desire

– Chris R. Powell

Alabaster White

November 17, 2020

My alabaster white,
my crimson red,
my royal purple,
my sapphire blue,
my emerald green,
my wonderful colors of every part of God's universe,
wrapped up in one beautiful jewel of a woman,
the most beautiful I have ever seen or
could imagine,
that he has given me,
now cast in a mutual love
now represented in two rings
that will forever be bound
together as our hearts are.

– Chris R. Powell

Oasis

March 10, 2021

Parched and dry in desert years
Parched and dry the days slide by
Blistering heat and pain and tears
Will the desert always be dry?

Shimmering on the edge of sand
shimmering under a Loki sun
Water glimmers, across the desert fanned
In glistening sheens, see the river run.

Is it once again a trick, a desert promise?
A mirage to melt in life's cruel heat?
It beckons me, offering bliss
Water cool, relief complete

The vision calls and on I go
Still doubting all I see
Yet here I feel the water flow
Cool upon my hands and feet

The palms loom high above my head
And shade—oh cool! – oh saving grace!
The cool blue waters shimmer ahead
And oh I know I've reached the place

At last of truth and grace
I sink into the shimmering pool
Into its cool embrace
Dive deep into the hidden jewel

That's love...that's love that holds at bay the strife
Oasis in the burning sands of life
Touch and cool my weary heart
Touch and cool my burning tongue

Oasis waters, you are love
That soothes the burning scorching sands
Oasis cool and shaded pool
That heals us from the journey's pains

Love, your waters lapping at my feet
Soothing in the desert sun
Love, your pools up to my knees
Refreshing from the battering sun

Oasis pool, Oasis love, wash and clean and heal

– Laura Vosika

The Swans Break, Broke, Deep

Pen—mother
Cob—father
Nest—home, form
Foundation strong
Every twig, intertwined,
Woven together, long

Eggs laid, long tended, broken form, gone
Each season, come again, each April, lonely song
Five long years, pattern repeated, five years long
All eggs shattered all eggs gone, all eggs gone

Pen—mother
Cob—father
Nest—home torn
Fireside burned down
Twigs long gone
Sweater by the table
Coffee still...*wrong*

Waking this morning
Sunrise different, colors seem...different
Keeping to myself
Skipping to the beat
On a different sidewalk
Looking to the heavens
Thinking on myself
Again…
Something seems different
Don't know what
Gotta keep it to myself

Pen—mother
Cob—father
Nest—home shorn
Phoenix reborn
Swans coming on back
Twigs building something
Don't know if I know what
Fabric seems stronger
Coming from something
Stronger deeper
Coming from my heart
Gotta keep it beating
Keep it goin
Keep it on a' coming
Coming from the Lord
I know it's right

Eggs in a basket, so many in the basket
How many in the basket? I know I can see
The Lord took five away from me
There are those in the basket
Those five in the basket
Plus none more and another one for me

Ten here for me and five up in Heaven
Ten her for me and five up in Heaven
Like dough in the oven
My soul is the leaven
Bread for my Lord, God

My heart, soul, and hands, God
My smile and my laughter
Guide me and mold me
These children of mine
And these children around me

All are gifts from you, Lord
These eggs in a basket
These gifts right from you, Lord
These blessings from Heaven
This dough in the oven
My soul is the leaven
Bread for my Lord, God
My heart, soul, and hands, God
My smile and my laughter
Guide me and mold me

These children of mine
And these children around me
All are gifts from you, Lord
These eggs in a basket

– Chris R. Powell

AFTERWORD

After some time apart, after dreams and visions, visitations from eagles, hawks, and swans, direct Word and Guidance, and what can only be described as miraculous incidence—circumstances brought us back Together in Laughter, Humor, Love, Romance, Butterflies, Forgiveness, Service, and Honor, and we were married on February 20, 2021, Laura's grandfather's birthday, witnessed before God by family and friends over music, food, laughter, and wine, as all such occasions should be witnessed. We said, "I do," with hands and hearts wrapped together as only two can who have loved over such a journey as ours, devoted to one another in ways that no one can tear asunder, knowing that God has intervened in both of our lives in a way that transcends time, multiple countries, and circumstances that can only be described as wondrous.

This book stands as testimony and Testament that such a path is real, that redemption and destiny are real, that love with a depth that is indescribable is real, and irrevocable faith underlying all of it is what creates Ties that Bind us in Sacrament to an Ever-Living God who redeems in Grace through Our Lord Jesus Christ, Amen and Amen, Salvator Mundi indeed. With this book, we say *Deus Gratias*, Thanks be to God.

We are now forever embarked on our joint journey, of love, yes, but so much more—of music, poetry, prose, publishing, reading our 5000 books, sharing, walking, hiking, our Irish wolfhound Liadan (and big dogs in general...), photography, laughter, making fun of almost anything, composition, family, faith, values, cooking, wine, movies ("No shtabbing!" *(Jo Jo Rabbit* rules...)), travel, camping, sunsets, sunrises, inventions, art, philosophy, teaching, and...anything else that excites both of us, which is pretty much almost *anything*

About the Authors

Dr. Chris Powell is an author, poet, musician, father, engineering and management consultant and aspiring polymath with his fingers on everything from fretboards and ivories to the pulse of post-modernism, surrealism, and nihilism's impact on the destruction of morality and sanity.

In April, 2015, Dr. Powell released his first book, *The Path that Shines,* a memoir of his late wife Bonnie's battle with a rare illness.

Laura Vosika is a mother, musician, author, editor, and poet. She is the author of *The Blue Bells Chronicles,* a tale of time travel, romance and redemption, ranging across modern and medieval Scotland. She has also written *Glenmirril Garden,* a collection of songs in Celtic styles; *Food & Feast in the World of the Blue Bells Chronicles: a gastronomic historic poetic musical romp in thyme*; and *Go Home and Practice,* a record book for learning efficient practice methods in music.

She co-hosts *Books & Brews with Laura Vosika and Michael Agnew,* a podcast that interviews a new author each month, pairing their work to brews!

Together, Chris and Laura have 10 children and 3 grandchildren. They collaborate on many projects, including the full-color photo book, *Poetry in Motion,* photography, and publishing; and writing, playing, and recording music.

Their current writing projects include the novels *The Saint in the Cellar* and *The Wedding,* and the non-fiction study of music, *The Theology of Music.*

Find more about their work at:

www.chrisandlaurapowell.com